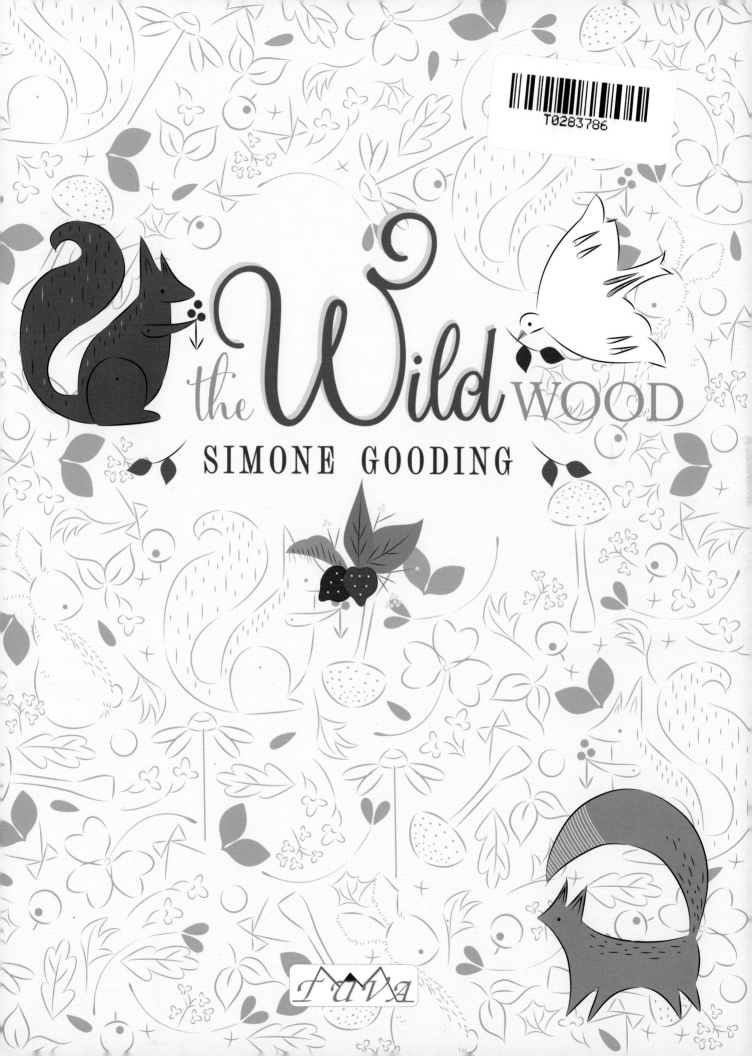

the Wild WOOD

SIMONE GOODING

Fava

Tuva Publishing

www.tuvapublishing.com

Address Merkez Mah. Cavusbasi Cad. No:71
Cekmekoy - Istanbul 34782 / Turkey
Tel: +9 0216 642 62 62

The Wild Wood

First Print 2023 / July

All Global Copyrights Belong To
Tuva Tekstil ve Yayıncılık Ltd.

Content Sewing

Editor in Chief Ayhan DEMİRPEHLİVAN
Project Editor Kader DEMİRPEHLİVAN
Designer Simone GOODING
Technical Editors Leyla ARAS
Graphic Designer Simone GOODING, Ömer ALP,
Abdullah BAYRAKÇI, Tarık TOKGÖZ,
Yunus GÜLDOĞAN

Photograph and Illustrations Simone GOODING

ISBN 978-605-7834-73-7

Contents

welcome to winter 7

materials & notions 10

haemostats 11

setting the eyes 14

PROJECTS

samphire 18

sweet pea 32

blackthorn forest brooches 42

birtwistle 48

62 roll of crayons

76 woodland heath mini quilt

82 hazel

102 wild strawberry pin cushion

templates 113

suppliers 128

the Wild WOOD

stitch all the beautiful festive

WINTER

inspired projects...

Welcome to Winter...

... and the lovely world of

the Wild WOOD

created by artist and illustrator Simone Gooding.

Containing a mixture of charming illustrations and photographs to help bring to life this gentle, quiet woodland community. In this craft book you will find a variety of festive, wintery animals and dolls with their accessories to stitch, knit and make.

Travel along through the Wild Woodland home of these friendly folk as they gather all they need to rug up warm.

You will find a small felt rabbit decoration with her velvet ruffled collar, a tiny mouse in her felt peapod zip up bed, three beautiful felt applique brooches, a red squirrel with her blue bird embroidered dress, tiny knitted dolls in their roll up felt pouch bed ... and much more.

With 100% wool hand dyed felt woodland characters and over 20 original knitted and fabric outfits and accessories 'The Wild Wood" provides all the inspiration and know-how needed to bring these beautiful characters to life.

Materials & Notions

100% wool hand dyed felt

I have been using Winterwood 100% wool hand dyed felt for many years now. It is very strong but also wonderfully soft so performs beautifully every time. In this book I have referenced names from their colour chart making it easier for you to use the exact same colours that I have used, if you so choose. I highly recommend you use very high quality wool felt, poor quality or synthetic felt will not withstand the small seam allowance, tight turning of pieces and firm stuffing required.

Buttons

For many years now I have been collecting vintage buttons. I just love to use vintage buttons, they have such wonderful colours, patterns and designs. My favourites are made of Bakelite Plastic from the 1940's and 50's. I have used a few from my collection in this book.

English glass doll making eyes

I just love this product! They are beautifully handmade and are very easy to use. They are jet black and have a little sheen on them which help to bring your toy animal/doll to life.

Jamieson's of Shetland yarn

I have been designing little sweaters, scarves, and hats for my toys for many years now. They are usually quite small in size so a gently fine yarn is needed. Once I found Jamieson's of Shetland's Spindrift I have not looked back. It is a 2 ply jumper fingering-weight yarn, which is equivalent to a 4 ply. It performs beautifully for small knitted items and has a wonderful, large range of colours in lovely muted, heathered tones.

Haemostats

Haemostats are a scissor type tool, with a clamp at the handle end. Instead of blades for cutting they have gripping teeth. Traditionally used in the medical field, they are a great addition to your sewing tool kit.

They come in many sizes. In this book I have used a small pair approximately 15cm (6") long with a pointy teeth end length of approximately 3cm (1 1/4"). They make the perfect tool for turning small limbs, ears etc when making toys and dolls.

To use the haemostats:

1. Open the teeth and slide them inside the leg, arm etc.

2. Pinch a small amount of the felt inside the teeth and clamp the scissor end.

3. Gently pull the haemostats, the felt piece will turn the correct way out.

4. They are also very useful for placing small amounts of stuffing into tiny areas.

SETTING THE EYES

1 Mark the position of the eyes with pins.

2 Cut a long piece of Gütterman Upholstery Thread and thread it through the metal loop at the back of the eye.

4 Take the needle off the thread and thread the needle again with only one length of the thread. Push the needle up through the stuffing and out of the face right next to one side of the eye. Repeat with the remaining thread on the other side of the eye.

3 Thread a long doll making needle with both ends of the thread, and push the needle through the front of the face at the position of the first pin. Bring the needle out in the stuffing at the neck.

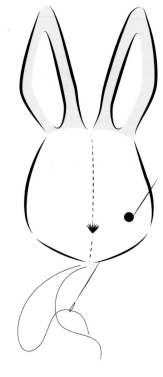

5 Take the two lengths of thread that are poking out on either side of the eye and tie a triple knot, pulling it tight so the knot is hidden behind the back of the eye.

6 Now thread the needle again with one of the lengths of thread and push the needle back in next to the eye and out through the stuffing in the neck. Repeat with the remaining thread.

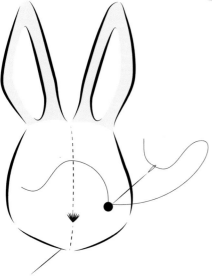

7 Tie a triple knot in the stuffing in the neck a few times until the eye is secure. Repeat steps 1-7 again with the remaining eye.

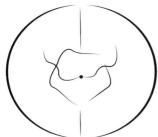

Ring Ouzel

Redstart

Redbreast

Hedge Sparrow

Wheater
Stonechat

Sedge Warbler

Reed Warbler

SAMPHIRE

head

1 Machine stitch around the head pieces leaving open where indicated at the base of the head. Leave the dart at the back of the head open at this stage.

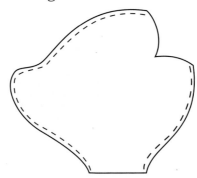

2 Position the gusset at the back of the head so that the seams match, machine stitch the gusset from edge to edge, Use the haemostats to help turn the head right side out, making sure to gently ease out all the curves.

3 Stuff the head until very firm with toy fill. The head circumference should measure approx. 13cm (5").

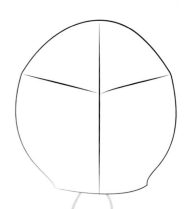

face

1 Mark the position for the eyes with pins. Following the eye setting instructions on page 14, attach the English glass eyes. Anchor your thread inside the stuffing in the head opening.

2 Using two strands of black embroidery thread, stitch a few backstitches over each other on the tip of the nose. Pass the thread back through the stitches and fasten off.

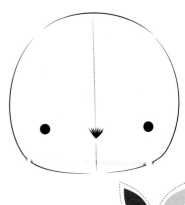

ears

1 Cut two ears from pale grey felt and two from the same colour felt as the body. Place them together in pairs each pair having one grey and one body colour.

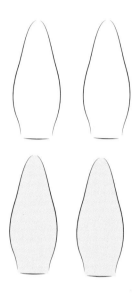

2 Machine stitch all the way around each ear leaving open where indicated. Use the haemostats to help turn the ears right side out, leaving the bottom straight edge open.

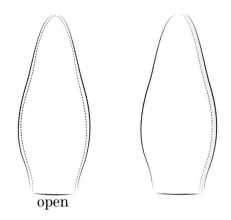

open

3 Cut approx. 15cm (6") length of pipe cleaner and fold it in half, gently mold the long sides of the pipe cleaner so they take on a slightly bowed 'V' shape.

4 Slide the pipe cleaner inside the ear and line up the pipe cleaner with the sides of the ear. Tuck under the raw open edge of the ear and stitch closed. Make a little fold in the straight end of each ear and hold with a small stitch.

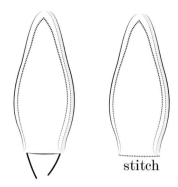

stitch

5 Pin the ears to the top, back part of the head, with the grey side to the back. Slightly curve the ears as you stitch them in place. The pipe cleaner will now allow you to mold the ears so they stay forward.

body

1 Machine stitch all the way around the body pieces leaving open where indicated at the back, leave the gusset at the base and top of the body open at this stage.

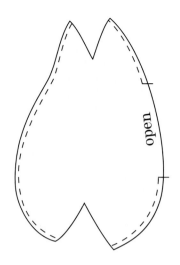

open

2 Position the gusset at the base of the body so that the seams match, machine stitch the gusset from edge to edge, repeat with the gusset at the top of the body.

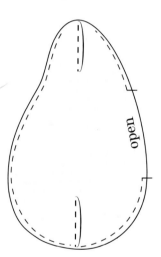

open

3 Turn right side out through the opening in the back, making sure to gently ease out all the curves and points.

4 Stuff the body until very firm with toy fill, hand stitch the body closed tucking in the raw edge as you stitch. The circumference around the middle of the body should measure approx. 14cm (5½").

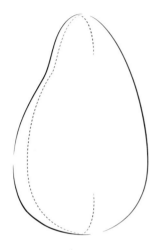

5 Make a little hollow in the stuffing in the head and push the top of the body inside the head opening quite firmly, making sure the neat seam on the front of the body lines up with the front of the head. Place pins in to hold tight while you stitch the head on to the body, stuff a little more as you stitch if needed so the head is firmly attached.

legs

1 Cut out four legs from matching felt. Place two legs together and stitch all the way around the leg and foot leaving open where indicated at the back of the leg.

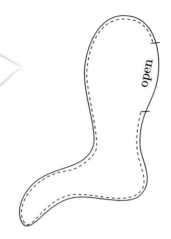

2 Use the haemostats to help turn each leg right side out. Stuff the whole leg well. Hand stitch the leg closed tucking in the raw edge as you stitch. Repeat with the remaining leg.

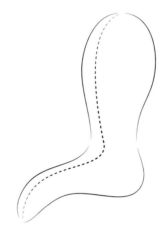

3 Pin the legs in place on each side of the body, and with two strands of the upholstery thread and a long doll making needle, stitch right through one leg through the body and out the other side of the other leg, keep going through in this fashion many times until the legs are firm, fasten off.

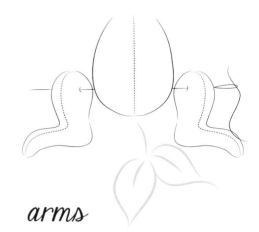

arms

1 Stitch the arms all the way around, leaving open where indicated.

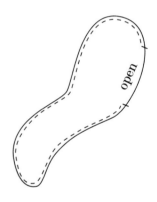

2 Turn right side out and stuff the arms firmly, close the openings on the arms.

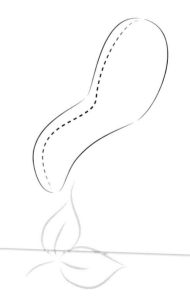

3 Pin the arms to each side of the body just under the head and with two strands of the upholstery thread and a long doll making needle, stitch right through one arm through the body and out the other side of the other arm, keep going through in this fashion many times until the arms are firm, fasten off.

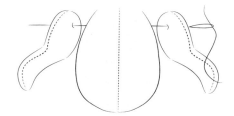

tail

1 Using matching thread to the felt gather by hand around the outer edge of the tail circle. Pull up the gathers so there is a small opening and fasten off but do not cut the thread yet. Stuff the tail until quite firm.

gather

2 Now stitch around the gathered circle again and pull the gathering until the opening is closed a little further.

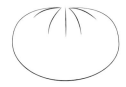

stitch

3 Stitch the tail to the back of the body.

ruffled ribbon collar

1 Cut a 20cm (8") piece of 5cm (2") wide velvet ribbon.

2 With right sides together, stitch the two short ends of the ribbon.

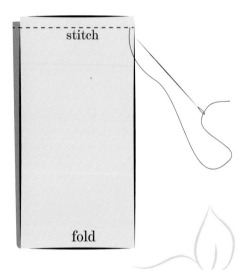

3 Open out the circle of ribbon and with wrong sides together, fold the ribbon in half so the edges of the ribbon meet.

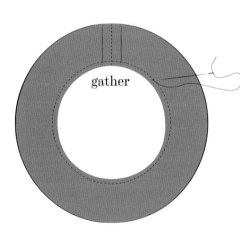

4 Using thread to match the ribbon, gather around the edge of the ribbon.

5 Place the circle of ribbon over the rabbit's head and with the seam of the ribbon at the back of the neck, pull up the gathers and fasten off.

knitted crown

1 Cast on 32 stitches.

2 Beginning with a knit row, stocking stitch 6 rows.

WORKING THE PICOT EDGE

3 Knit 2 together, yarn to the end of the row.

4 Beginning with a purl row, stocking stitch 6 rows.

5 Cast off purl wise.

making up

1 Using Mattress stitch, stitch the row ends together.

2 Fold the piece in half so the points of the Picot Edge poke through. Stitch the cast on and cast off edges together. *the cast on edge will be on the outside of the crown.

3 Stitch the small pearl beads in place on each point of the crown.

4 Place the crown on to the rabbit's head, tilting to one side and with one ear poking out through the centre of the crown. Stitch in place on to the head.

5 Cut approx. 25cm (10") cream Perle thread, make a loop and stitch it to the top of the head for hanging.

carrot

1 Cast on 5 stitches.

2 Beginning with a purl row, stocking stitch 5 rows.

3 Increase knitwise into every stitch – 10 stitches.

4 Beginning with a purl row, stocking stitch 20 rows.

5 Cut the yarn from the ball, leaving a long length. Thread a bodkin with the length and thread it through the 20 stitches on the knitting needle.

making up

1 Beginning at the cast on edge of the carrot, thread the long length of yarn on to a bodkin. Mattress stitch the row ends together all the way up to the top.

2 Stuff the carrot gently, lay aside for now.

3 Wrap a long length of green yarn around two fingers approx. 10 times.

4 Take the yarn off your fingers and wrap yarn around the loops at one end. Pull the yarn firmly.

5 Push the ends of the loops into the top of the carrot, pull up the gathers in the top edge of the carrot and fasten off.

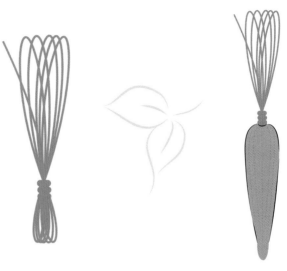

6 Bring the little hands to the front of the body and add a few stitches to hold, place the carrot in the cradled arms.

SWEET PEA

you will need

- 6" x 6" (15cm x 15cm) 'Mist' 100% wool hand dyed felt for head, ears and tail
- 3" x 4" (8cm x 10cm) 'Cream' 100% wool felt for body
- 3.5" x 3.5" (9cm x 9cm) fabric for ears and body detail
- 14" (35cm) cotton twine for ears and tail
- Small pair of Haemostats.
- x2 4mm black English glass doll eyes
- Black embroidery thread
- Long doll making needle
- Gutermann Upholstery thread to match the felt
- Sewing machine thread to match the felt
- Toy fill
- General sewing supplies

* 3mm (⅛") seam allowance included

* templates on page 115

* finished size 12.5cm (5")

head

1 Machine stitch around the head pieces leaving open where indicated at the base of the head. Leave the dart at the back of the head open at this stage.

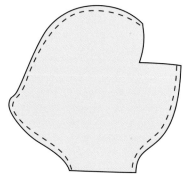

2 Position the gusset at the back of the head so that the seams match, machine stitch the gusset from edge to edge, Use the haemostats to help turn the head right side out, making sure to gently ease out all the curves.

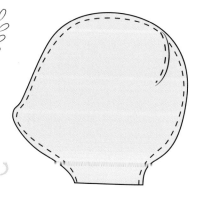

3 Stuff the head until very firm with toy fill. The head circumference should measure approx. 14cm (5.5")

face

1 Mark the position for the eyes with pins. Following the eye setting instructions on page 14, attach the English glass eyes. Anchor your thread inside the stuffing in the head opening.

2 Using two strands of black embroidery thread, stitch a few backstitches over each other on the tip of the nose. Pass the thread back through the stitches and fasten off.

ears

1 Cut two ears from pale grey felt and two from fabric. Place them together in pairs each pair having one grey and one fabric.

2 Machine stitch all the way around each ear leaving open where indicated along the bottom edge.

open

3 Turn the ears right side out. Turn under the raw open edge and hand stitch closed.

stitch

4 Pin the ears to the top, back part of the head, with the grey felt side to the back. Slightly curve the ears as you stitch them in place.

5 Cut approx. 14" (35 cm) of twine into three equal lengths. Make three tiny bows, two for the ears and set one bow aside for later for the end of the tail. Place the bows in front of each ear and add a few stitches to hold them in place.

body

1 Using a ¼" bias tape maker, make the following fabric strips:

      x1 - 3.5" long piece
      x1 - 2" long piece

2 Place the bias strips on top of one of the body pieces and top stitch them in place as shown.

3 Snip the raw ends of the strips in line with the body edges.

4 With right sides together, machine stitch all the way around the body pieces leaving open where indicated at the top straight edge. Turn right side out and stuff until firm.

open

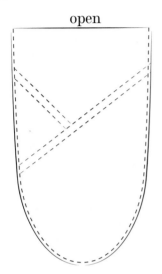

5 Gather by hand around the top straight open edge.

gather

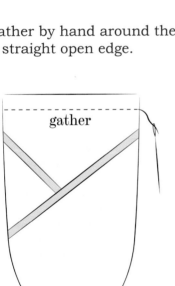

6 Pull up the gathers tight and fasten off.

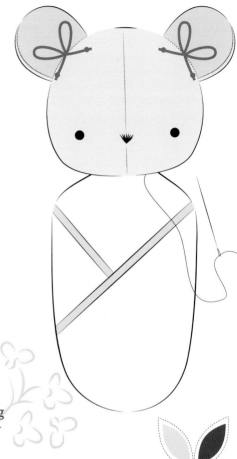

7 Push the top gathered edge of the body inside the opening in the head. Using upholstery thread Stitch the head on firmly.

tail

1 Fold the tail in half lengthwise and machine stitch all the way down the length. Hand stitch the wider end of the tail to the bottom tucking in a tiny raw edge as you stitch.

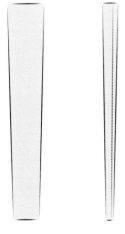

2 Stitch the extra bow you made earlier to the tip of the tail.

3 Curve the tail to the front of the body and hand stitch in place.

PEAPOD

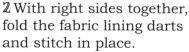

~ you will need ~

. 10" x 4" (26cm x 10cm) 'Moss' 100% wool felt for peapod

. 10" x 4" (26cm x 10cm) fabric for peapod lining

. 6" (15cm) zipper

. 14" (35cm) cotton twine

. Sewing machine thread to match the felt

. General sewing supplies

* 5mm (¼") seam allowance included

* templates on page 116

* finished size 22cm (9")

peapod

1 Fold the darts on the felt pieces and stitch.

2 With right sides together, fold the fabric lining darts and stitch in place.

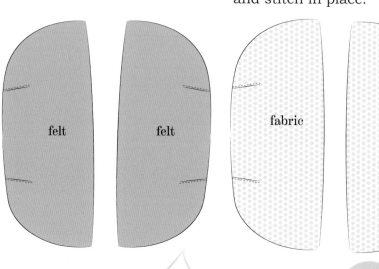

zipper

1 Take one felt piece and place it on your work surface right side up. Place the zipper in the centre with its right side down on top of the felt piece, keeping the upper edges together. Now place one lining piece on top of the zipper right side down.

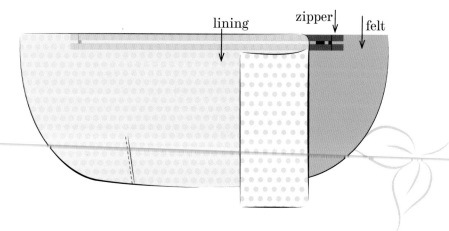

2 Stitch along the upper edge using a ¼" seam allowance, making sure to let the ends of the zipper poke out of the seams.

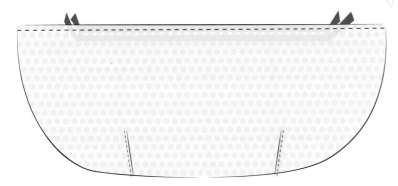

3 Press the lining piece back from the zipper, (don't press the felt piece yet) and top stitch the lining in place against the zipper. Now press the felt piece back from the zipper.

4 Repeat steps 1 and 2 on the opposite side of the zipper, with the remaining felt and lining pieces.

5 Open the zipper, with both lining pieces together and both felt pieces together, machine stitch all the way around the piece, leaving a small turning gap in the lining.

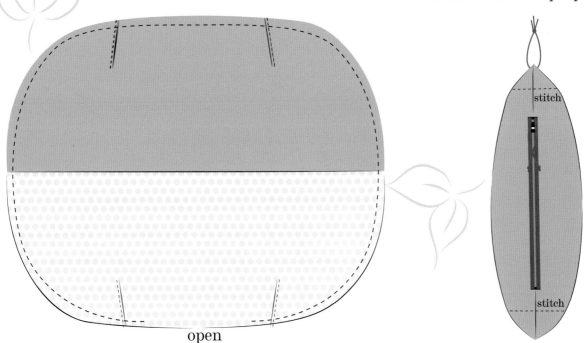

open

6 Turn the piece right side out and press. Hand stitch the opening in the lining closed.

7 Tuck the lining to the inside and press well.

8 Hand stitch the open ends of the pea pod.

9 Machine top stitch both ends flat.

10 Cut a 10" (25cm) piece of twine, fold it in half and knot the ends. Hand stich the loop to one end of the peapod.

11 Cut 4" (10cm) of twine and thread it through the end of the zipper pull, knot to secure.

Blackthorn Forest

brooches

BLACKTHORN FOREST BROOCHES

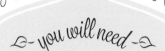

you will need

- 4" x 4" (10cm x 10cm) 100% wool, hand dyed felt for each brooch background colour

- Small scraps of desired 100% wool hand dyed felt colours for applique

- Assorted seed beads

- Black embroidery thread

- Matching and contrasting embroidery threads

- Small safety pin

- Applique pins

- General sewing supplies

* all brooches use blanket stitch, backstitch, and French knots. The Red Squirrel brooch is demonstrated with diagrams.

* templates on page 117

* finished diameter 7cm (2 3/4")

brooches

1 Using small scraps of 100% wool, hand dyed felt. Cut out the desired applique pieces and the background piece. Using the placement guide, (page 118) position the pieces and use applique pins to hold in place.

2 Using two strands of matching embroidery thread, blanket stitch around the outer edge of each piece. Use a contrasting colour thread to hand stitch long backstitches and French knots on the back and tail.

3 Use the placement guide to stitch backstitches for the leaves and tiny seed beads in place for the berries.

4 For the red squirrel and dove, use four strands of black embroidery thread to stitch a French knot in place for the eye.

5 Cut a second background piece to match the first one you cut; this will be for the back of the brooch.

6 Using two strands of matching thread, stitch a small safety pin to the back of the second background piece.

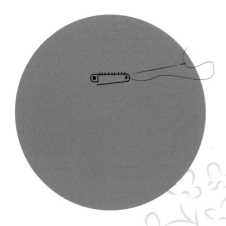

7 With wrong sides facing, place the background pieces together. Using two strands of matching thread to blanket stitch all the way around the outer edge of both pieces.

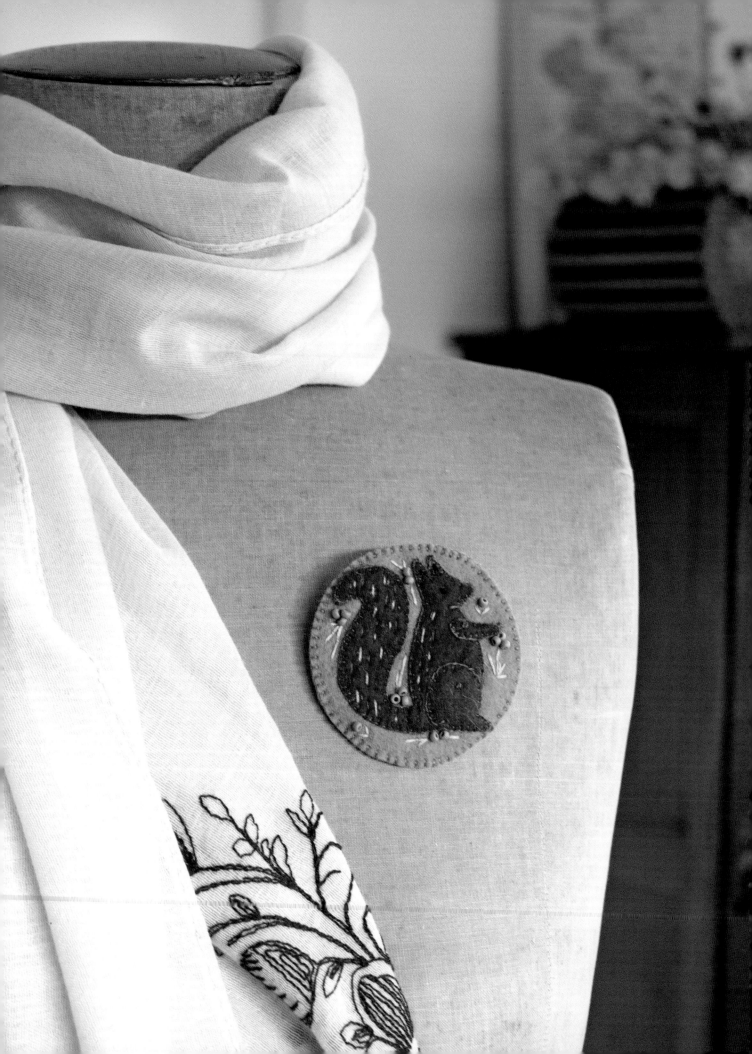

Birtwistle

BIRTWISTLE

head

1 Fold one head piece in half along the fold line down the centre of the head, machine stitch along both gusset seams, repeat with the remaining head piece.

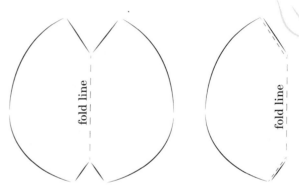

fold line

fold line

2 Open out the two headpieces and with right sides of the heads facing and the top and bottom gussets matching, stitch around the outer edge of the head, leaving open at the bottom where indicated.

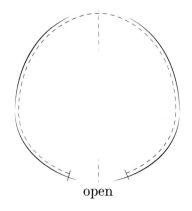

open

3 Turn the head right side out and stuff very firmly. The head circumference should measure approx. 30.5cm (12").

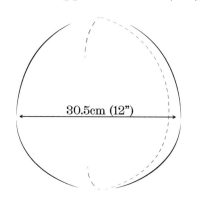

30.5cm (12")

4 Cut two circles from tan felt for the eye patches. Position them as marked on the head and using two strands of matching embroidery thread, blanket stitch them in place.

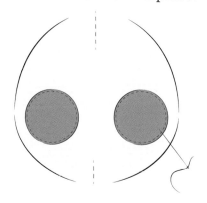

eyes

1 Mark the position for the eyes with pins. Following the eye setting instructions on page 14, attach the English glass eyes. Anchor your thread inside the stuffing in the head opening.

2 Using two strands each of dark brown, peach, tan, mushroom coloured embroidery thread, add long, random back stitches to the face as shown, fastening your thread in the opening of the head.

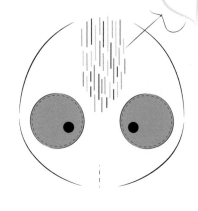

beak

1 Place the two beak pieces together and machine stitch around the curved edge, turn right side out and stuff a little.

open

2 Using two strands of black embroidery thread, stitch two French knots in place on the top of the beak as shown.

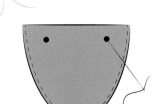

3 Pin the beak in place on the face so the open edge of the beak is between the tan circles. Using matching thread, hand stitch the beak in place tucking in the raw edge as you go.

body

1 Cut one body piece from cream felt and one from dark brown felt. Place the two body pieces together and machine stitch down the side seams and along the bottom edge, leave the square corner shapes unsewn for now.

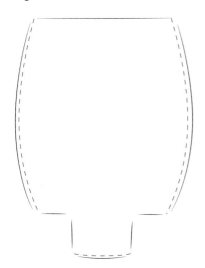

2 Bring the corners of the square corner shape together so the side seam and the bottom seam match, this will make a straight edge, stitch along this edge with the same tiny seam allowance. Repeat with the remaining square corner.

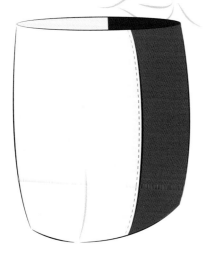

3 Turn the body right side out and gently push out the corners. Using two strands of matching embroidery thread, gather by hand around the top open edge of the body.

4 Fill the body to approx. a third with teddy stuffing pellets and then stuff the remainder with toy fill until quite firm. The body should measure approx. 33cm (13"). Pull up the gathers so the top edge of the body just curves in and fasten the stitches off. Push more stuffing in if needed.

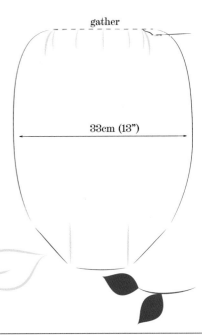

gather

33cm (13")

5 In the same way as for the head, use the coloured embroidery threads to make long random backstitches down the cream front of the body.

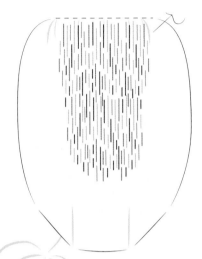

6 Turning the head to the left, place the head on top of the body. Place pins in to hold tight while you stitch the head on to the body with upholsery thread. Stuff a little more into the body as you stitch if needed so the head is firmly attached.

wings

1 Cut four wing shapes, two from cream felt and two from dark brown felt.

2 Place the dark brown set on a tabletop with the curved edges facing in, place the cream set on top of the dark brown set and machine stitch all the way around each set, leaving open where indicated.

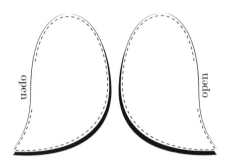

3 Clip the corner, turn right side out and press. Hand stitch the opening closed.

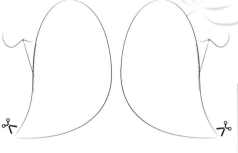

4 Cut approx. 18 wing feathers from small scraps of cream, peach, tan, rusty red and chocolate brown felt.

5 Beginning at the bottom of one wing, on the dark brown side, machine stitch each feather in place down the centre. Making sure to slightly overlap each feather

as you stitch and to place the colours randomly.

6 Hand stitch each wing in place to each side of the body, with the pointed end of each wing facing the back.

53

KNITTED HAT

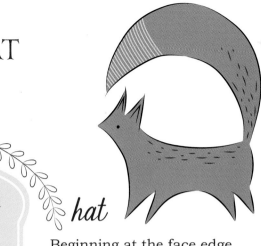

you will need

hat

. 3.25mm (3¼) knitting
   needles
. Jamieson's Shetland
   Spindrift 4 ply yarn: in
   the following colours:
      Hat:
         Mogit - 107
      Swiss Darning:
         Foxglove – 273
         Orchid – 547
         Moss – 147
         Buttercup - 182
. Bodkin

violet

. 100% wool hand dyed felt:
   . 5" x 3" (13cm x 7.5cm)
      'Iris'
   . 3.5" x 3" (9cm x 7.5cm)
      'Daintree'
. Yellow Perle Cotton thread

. General sewing supplies

* violet templates on
   page 121

hat

Beginning at the face edge,
cast on 58 stitches.

Garter stitch 6 rows, slipping
the first stitch knitwise on
every row.

* Begin stocking stitch

1 Slip the first stitch knitwise,
knit to the end of the row.

2 Slip the first stitch knitwise,
knit 2, purl to the last 3
stitches, knit 3.

* Repeat these two rows 11
more times.

shaping the back

1 Slip the first stitch knitwise,
knit 18, knit 2 together 10
times, knit 19
– 48 stitches.

2 Garter stitch 5 rows, slipping
the first stitch knitwise on
every row.

3 Slip first stitch knitwise,
knit 13, knit 2 together 10
times, knit 14
– 38 stitches.

4 Garter stitch 3 rows, slipping
the first stitch knitwise on
every row.

5 Slip the first stitch knitwise,
knit 8, knit 2 together 10
times, knit 9
– 28 stitches.

6 Cast off.

* Block the piece by laying
a piece of kitchen towel over
it and using a cool iron to
steam. Allow the piece to dry.

collar piece

* Begin at lower edge, cast on
64 stitches.

1 Garter stitch 6 rows, slipping
the 1st stitch knitwise on
every row.

2 Beginning with a knit row, stocking stitch 8 rows – knit the 1st 4 stitches and the last 4 stitches on every purl row.

3 Knit 1, knit 2 together to the end of the row
– 43 stitches

4 Cast off.

* Block the piece by laying a piece of kitchen towel over it and using a cool iron to steam. Allow the piece to dry.

making up

1 Thread the length of yarn on to a bodkin. Fold the cast off edge of the hat in half and mattress stitch across the cast off edge. Weave in the ends of any remaining yarn. Fasten off.

2 Using matching yarn, lightly gather across the cast off edge of the collar.

3 Mattress stitch the cast off edge to the bottom edge of the hat.

twisted tie

Make two in total

1 Cut two 60cm (23.5") lengths of matching yarn.

2 Tape the two ends to a tabletop and twist the yarn until it is very firm.

3 Remove from the tabletop and fold the piece in half and let it twist back on itself. Smooth it out and knot the ends together.

4 Stitch each folded end to the front corners of the hat, where the collar and the hat meet.

embroidery - duplicate stitch

1 Using one length of desired yarn colour, follow the chart to duplicate stitch (Swiss darning) the extra designs to the hat.

I have used a slightly blunt nosed needle, as opposed to a sharp needle. A sharp needle can split the fibres of the yarn.

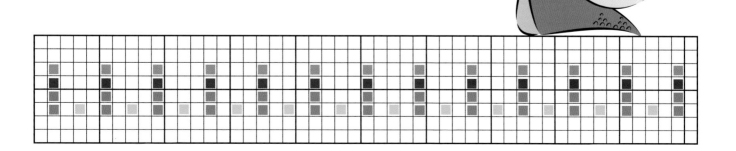

violet

1 Cut out 8 petals from violet coloured felt. Take three petals and using matching coloured embroidery thread, gather along the straight edge of each petal, threading one after the other on to the thread until you have three petals gathered along the thread. Pull them tightly and fasten off, lay aside for now.

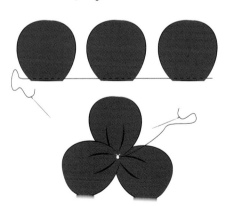

2 Repeat this process with the remaining five petals, now place the first three petals

on top of the five and add a few stitches to hold them together.

3 Using two strands of bright yellow Perle cotton, stitch a French knot in the centre of the violet.

leaves

1 Cut out 2 leaves from deep green felt. Using a slightly lighter shade of green thread on your sewing machine, stitch a straight line of stitching through the centre of each leaf.

2 Hand stitch one point of the leaves in place on the back of the violet.

3 Stitch the violet in place on the left corner of the knitted hat.

ROLL UP POUCH

~ you will need ~

. 20½" x 7½" (52cm x 19cm) 'Cloudears' 100% wool hand dyed felt for pouch.

. 51" (130cm) 1" bias tape

. 4" (10cm) thin elastic

. x1 small vintage/novelty button

. Quilter's mat

. Rotary cutter

. General sewing supplies

* *5mm (¼") seam allowance included*

* *finished size 52cm x 11cm (20¹/₄ x 4¹/₄)*

* *no templates required*

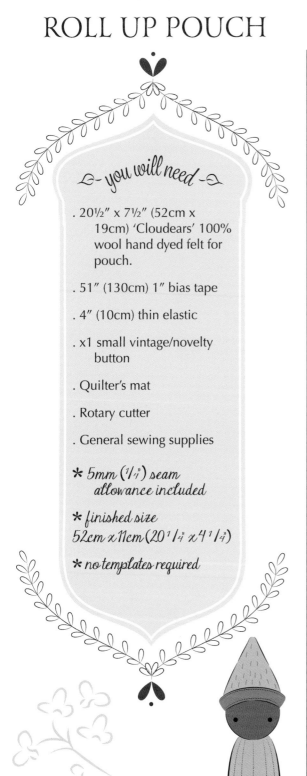

roll up pouch

1 Using your quilter's mat and rotary cutter, cut a piece of 100% wool hand dyed felt for the roll up pouch that measures 20½" x 7½" (52cm x 19cm).

2 Cut approx. 20½" (52cm) of 1" bias tape. Open it out and with right sides together and using a ¼" seam allowance, stitch one long raw edge of the tape to one long raw edge of the pouch piece.

20.5" x 7.5" (52cm x 19cm)

3 Press the tape up and over to the wrong side of the pouch piece and hand stitch the bias tape in place.

4 Fold up the bias tape edge of the pouch piece approx. 3" (8cm). The bias tape will now form the neat top edge of the pouches.

3" (8cm)

5 Measure the centre of the piece and mark with a pin. Now from this centre point, mark 2.5" (6½ cm) increments. There will be eight in total.

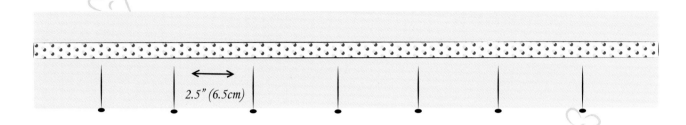

2.5" (6.5cm)

6 Machine top stitch each pouch section.

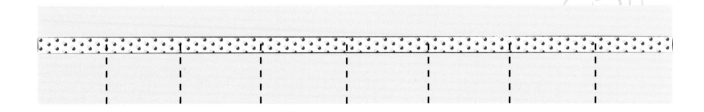

7 Take the remaining length of bias tape. Beginning at the bottom side edge, open it out and with right sides together and using a ¼" seam allowance, stitch the tape all the way around the remaining pouch outer edge.

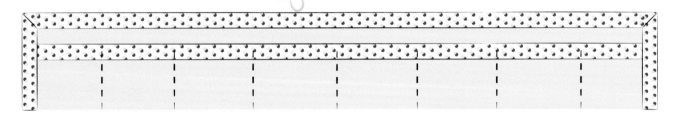

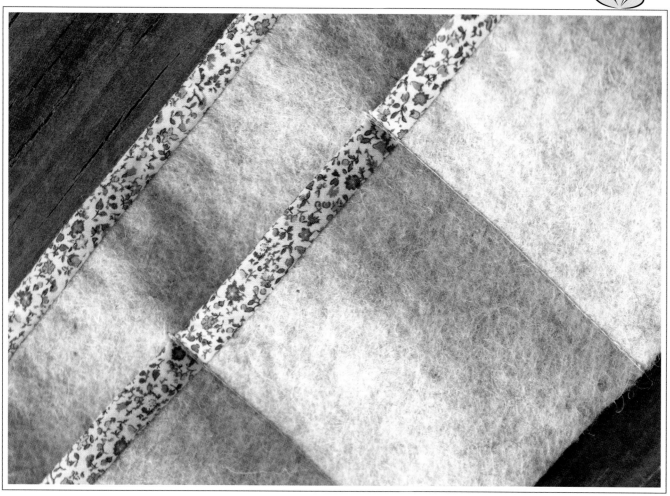

8 Cut a 4" (10cm) piece of thin elastic. Fold it in half and knot together to form a loop. Hand stitch the loop to the back, on one side edge.

back

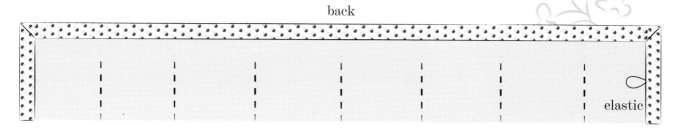

elastic

9 Press the bias tape to the back of the pouch and hand stitch the tape in place.

10 Count along to the stitching between the 5th and 6th pouch and stitch a small vintage/novelty button in place on top of the pouch stitching.

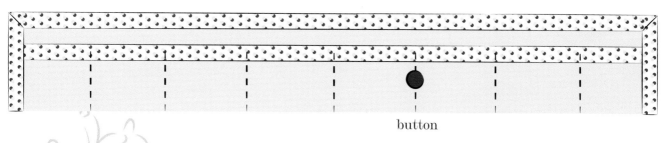

button

CRAYON KNITTED DOLL

you will need

. Jamieson's Shetland
  Spindrift 4 ply yarn: in
  the following colours:

  Sunglow – 185

  Dogrose – 268

  Scotchbroom – 1160

  Buttermilk – 179

  Apple – 785

  Prairie – 812

  Blue Danube – 134

  Foxglove – 273

. x8 2½cm diameter wool
  felt balls in various flesh
  shades
. Black Perle thread
. 3mm knitting needles
. Bodkin
. Toy fill
. General sewing supplies

* *finished size 11.5cm (4¹⁄₂)*

* *no templates required*

body

Beginning at the neck edge.

1 Cast on 10 stitches.

2 Increase knitwise into every
stitch – 20 stitches.

3 Beginning with a purl row,
stocking stitch 25 rows.

4 Knit 2 together to the end of the
row – 10 stitches.

5 Cut the yarn from the ball,
leaving a long length. Thread a
bodkin with the length and thread
it through the 10 stitches on the
knitting needle, pull gently until
firm.

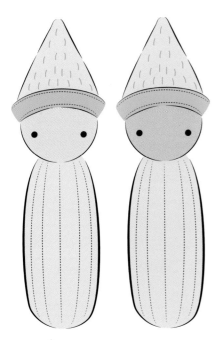

making up

1 Thread the long length of yarn on to a bodkin. Mattress stitch the row ends together all the way up to the neck edge. Weave in the ends of any remaining yarn. Fasten off.

2 Stuff the body until it measures approx. 3¼" (8½cm) around the middle.

little crayon hat

Beginning at the brim edge.

1 Cast on 24 stitches.

2 Knit row.

3 Knit row.

4 Purl row.

5 Knit row.

6 Purl row.

7 k1, knit 2 together (8 times) – 16 stitches.

8 Purl row.

9 k1, knit 2 together (5 times) k1 – 11 stitches.

10 Purl row.

11 k1, knit 2 together (3 times) k2 – 8 stitches.

12 Purl row.

13 Knit 2 together (4 times) – 4 stitches.

14 Cut the yarn from the ball, leaving a long length. Thread a bodkin with the length and thread it through the 4 stitches on the knitting needle, pull gently until firm.

making up

1 Thread the long length of yarn on to a bodkin. Mattress stitch the row ends together all the way up to the brim edge.

2 Use the length of yarn to stitch the little crayon hat to the top of a felt ball.

3 Take a length of black Perle thread. Stitch two French knots in place for the eyes. (Fasten your thread at the base of the felt ball, so it will be hidden once you stitch the body on).

4 Stitch the knitted body in place on the base of the felt ball. Tuck your dolls snuggly in their pouches, roll up and fasten.

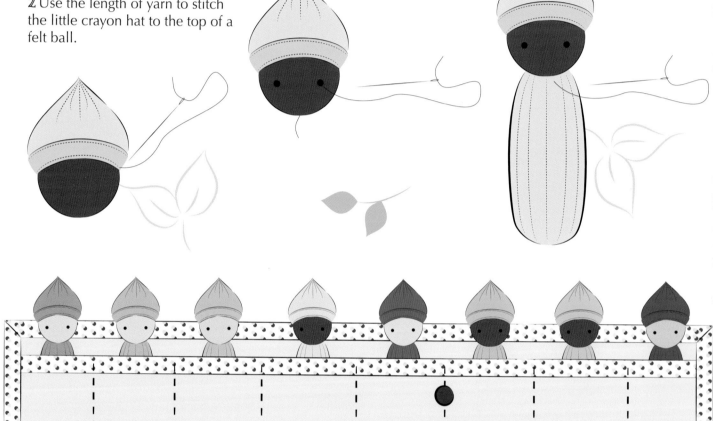

73

Woodland Heath

mini quilt

WOODLAND HEATH MINI QUILT

felt quilt top

1 Trace and cut out the quilt top on to a piece of paper, making sure to carefully cut out all the leaf shapes.

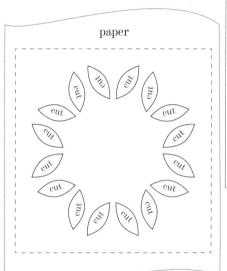

2 Place the pattern piece on top of your 9" x 9" (23cm x 23cm) piece of 100% wool hand dyed felt. Pin in place with tiny applique pins and using small sharp scissors, cut out the felt leaf shapes.

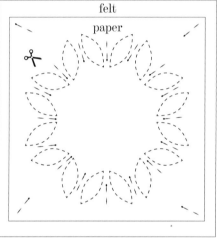

3 Using the leaf pattern piece, cut out 16 leaves using an array of different fabrics.

4 Place your leaves right side down on to one side of your felt quilt top, making sure to accurately place each leaf so it covers over one of your cut outs.

5 Cut a piece of light weight, iron on batting that measures 9" x 9" (23cm x 23cm). Carefully place it glue side down on top of the fabric leaf shapes. Gently press it with your iron. This will help to hold the leaves in position.

iron on batting

6 Cut a piece of linen/fabric for the backing that measures 9" x 9" (23cm x 23cm). Place it on top of the batting. Turn the piece over so you can see the front, clip or pin the layers together while you top stitch around the leaf shapes.

7 Using a rotary cutter, quilter's ruler and mat, trim your mini quilt so it measures 8"x 8" (20cm x 20cm).

8 Bind the mini quilt with the ¾" bias tape, open out the tape and using the crease as a guide, stitch the tape to the front of the mini quilt, keeping raw edges even and mitring the corners. Fold the tape to the back and hand stitch in place.

Hazel

HAZEL

~ you will need ~

. 100% wool hand dyed felt:
. 18" x 16.5" (46cm x 42cm) 'Wattlebark' for squirrel
. 5.5" x 2.5" (14cm x 6cm) 'Dingo' for inner ears
. 5" x 3" (12cm x 8cm) 'Blueberry' for flowers
. 5" x 3" (12cm x 8cm) 'Daintree' for leaves
. 16.5" x 12.5" (42cm x 32cm) 16 count Aida fabric for cross stitch
. Blue embroidery thread
. Embroidery needle
. x2 6mm black English glass doll eyes
. Black embroidery thread
. Yellow Perle Cotton thread
. 50cm (20") piece of decorative ribbon for fastening the dress
. 3.25mm knitting needles
. Jamieson's Shetland Spindrift 4 ply yarn: in the following colours:
   Dogrose - 268
   Buttermilk - 179
. Decorative/vintage button for shawl and bag
. Long doll making needle.
. Gütermann Upholstery thread to match the felt
. Sewing machine thread to match the felt
. Bodkin
. Toy fill
. General sewing supplies

* *3mm (⅛") seam allowance included for squirrel*
* *5mm (¼") seam allowance included for dress*
* *templates on page 123-125*
* *finished size 28cm (11")*

head

1 Machine stitch around the head pieces leaving open where indicated at the base of the head. Leave the dart at the back of the head open at this stage.

2 Position the gusset at the back of the head so that the seams match, machine stitch the gusset from edge to edge, turn the head right side out, making sure to gently ease out all the curves.

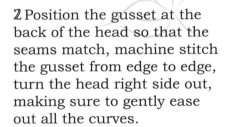

3 Stuff the head until very firm with toy fill. The head circumference should measure approx. 26cm (10¼").

face

1 Mark the position for the eyes with pins. Following the eye setting instructions on page 14, attach the English glass eyes. Anchor your thread inside the stuffing in the head opening.

2 Using two strands of black thread stitch two back stitches in place as the eyelashes. Using 2 strand of black embroidery thread, stitch two backstitches either side of the pointed nose and one long back underneath, along the seam.

ears

1 Cut two ears from caramel felt and two from the same colour felt as the body. Place them together in pairs each pair having one caramel and one body colour.

2 Machine stitch all the way around each ear leaving open where indicated, turn the ears right side out, leaving the bottom straight edge open.

open

3 Make a little fold in the straight end of each ear and hold with a small stitch.

4 Pin the ears in place on top of the head making sure the folded front of each ear faces to the side of the head. Stitch the ears in place tucking in a small raw edge as you stitch.

body

1 Machine stitch all the way around the body pieces leaving open where indicated at the back, leave the dart at the base of the body open at this stage.

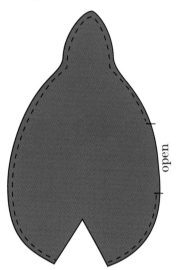

open

2 Position the dart at the base of the body so that the seams match, machine stitch the dart from edge to edge, turn right side out through the opening in the back, making sure to gently ease out all the curves and points.

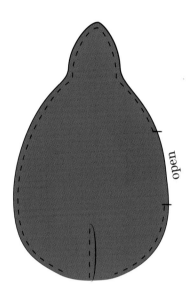

3 Stuff the body until very firm with toy fill, hand stitch the body closed tucking in the raw edge as you stitch. The circumference around the middle of the body should measure approx. 23cm (9").

4 Make a little hollow in the stuffing in the head and push the top of the body inside the head opening quite firmly, making sure the neat seam on the front of the body lines up with the front of the head. Place pins in to hold tight while you stitch the head on to the body, stuff a little more as you stitch if needed so the head is firmly on the body.

legs

1 Cut out four legs from matching felt. Place two legs together and stitch all the way around the leg and foot leaving open where indicated at the back of the leg.

2 Turn right side out and stuff the whole leg well. Hand stitch the leg closed tucking in the raw edge as you stitch. Repeat with the remaining leg.

3 Pin the legs in place on each side of the body, and with two strands of the upholstery thread and a long doll making needle, stitch right through one leg through the body and out the other side of the other leg, keep going through in this fashion many times until the legs are firm, fasten off.

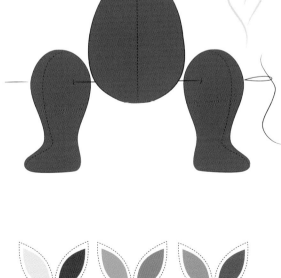

arms

1 Stitch the arms all the way around, leaving open where indicated.

2 Turn right side out and stuff the arms firmly, close the openings on the arms.

3 Pin the arms to each side of the body just under the head and with two strands of the upholstery thread and a long doll making needle, stitch right through one arm through the body and out the other side of the other arm, keep going through in this fashion many times until the arms are firm, fasten off.

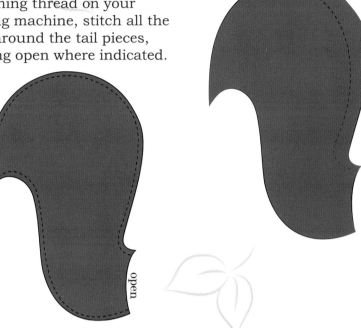

tail

1 Cut two tail pieces, using matching thread on your sewing machine, stitch all the way around the tail pieces, leaving open where indicated.

open

2 Turn right side out and stuff firmly.

forget me not flowers

1 Cut 12 flowers from pale blue felt and four leaves from leaf green felt.

2 Take two leaves and overlap them at one end. Add a few stitches to hold in place. Stitch this end just behind one ear.

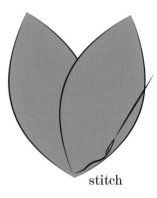

stitch

3 Position six of the blue flowers in place around one ear just in front of the leaves and slightly overlapping the flowers. Using two strands of yellow Perle cotton, fix each flower in place with a French Knot in the centre. Repeat with the remaining leaves and flowers.

3 Stitch the tail to the back of the body.

dress

1 Using a rotary cutter, quilter's ruler and mat cut the following from your 16 count Aida fabric for cross stitch.

X1 12" x 10" dress front   X2 12" x 3" dress backs

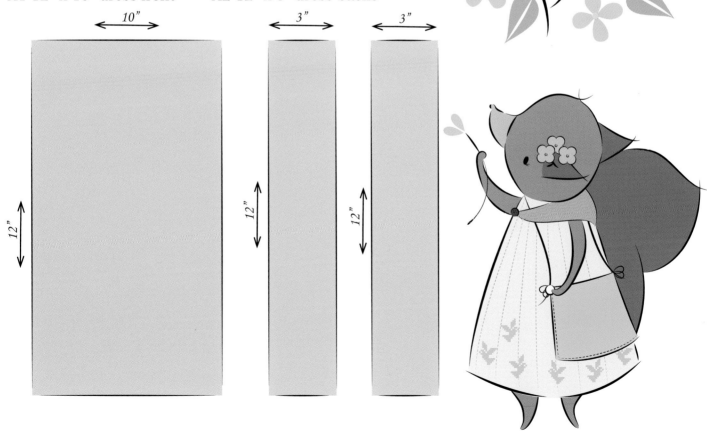

2 Tape around the edges of all three pieces with masking tape to stop the fabric fraying while you stitch the blue bird design.

3 Fold the dress front piece in half, and finger press to find the centre. Open out again and using the blue bird cross stitch design, and two strands of blue embroidery thread, stitch the blue birds in place, just above the crease.

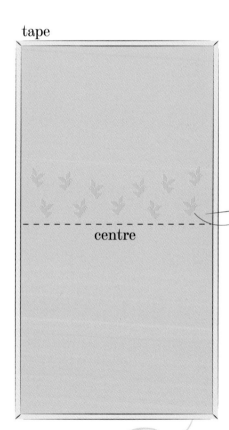

tape

centre

4 Take one of the dress back pieces, fold it in half and finger press to find the centre. Open out again and using the blue bird cross stitch design, and two strands of blue embroidery thread, stitch the blue birds in place, just above the crease. Repeat with the remaining dress back piece.

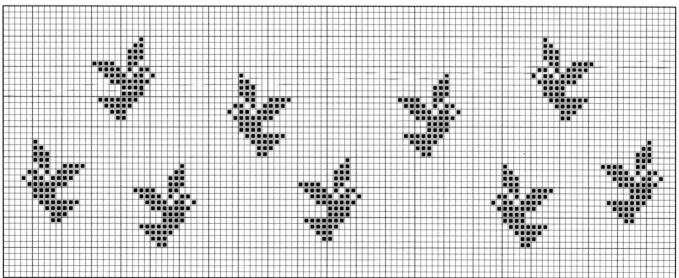

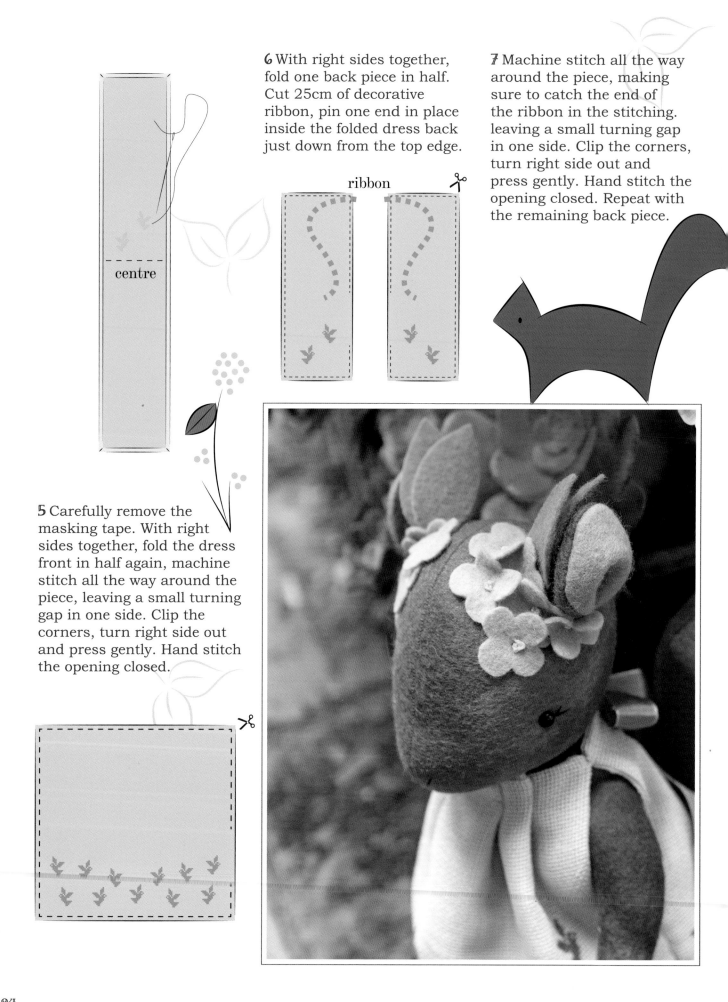

6 With right sides together, fold one back piece in half. Cut 25cm of decorative ribbon, pin one end in place inside the folded dress back just down from the top edge.

ribbon

7 Machine stitch all the way around the piece, making sure to catch the end of the ribbon in the stitching. leaving a small turning gap in one side. Clip the corners, turn right side out and press gently. Hand stitch the opening closed. Repeat with the remaining back piece.

centre

5 Carefully remove the masking tape. With right sides together, fold the dress front in half again, machine stitch all the way around the piece, leaving a small turning gap in one side. Clip the corners, turn right side out and press gently. Hand stitch the opening closed.

❽ Make a small 3cm pleat along the top edge in the centre front of the dress front piece. Hold with clips or pins. Make two 1cm pleats either side of the centre pleat and hold with clips or pins. Hand stitch the pleats in place.

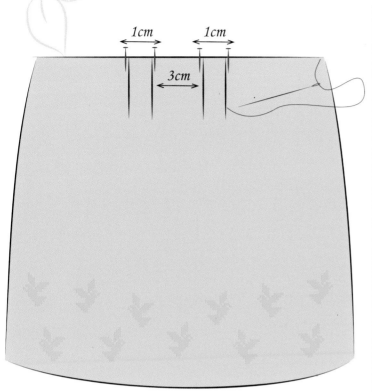

❾ Make a 1cm pleat in the top edge of one dress back piece. Hand stitch in place and repeat with the remaining dress back.

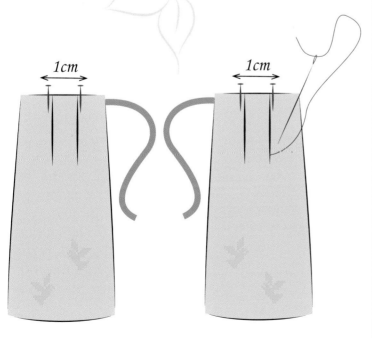

10 Beginning at the hem end, hand stitch one side edge of the dress front to the side edge (without the ribbon) of the dress back, approx. 5.5cm (2¼") up from the hem edge.

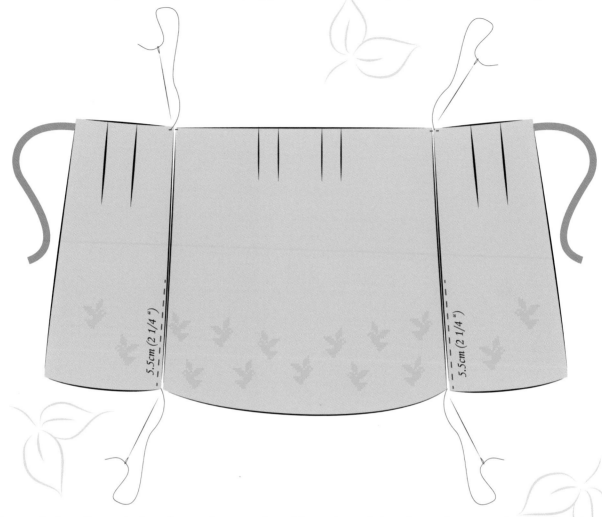

11 Now stitch a few stitches in at the top shoulder edge of the dress front and dress back. Repeat step 10 and 11 on the remaining dress back.

12 Place the dress on to Hazel, passing her arms through the gaps in the side seams. Fasten at the back with the ribbon.

shawl

1 Cast on 2 stitches

2 Work in garter stitch and increase 2 stitches at the beginning of the first and every following row until there are 12 stitches.

3 (Continue increasing 2 stitches at the beginning of each row)

4 Work 5 garter stitches at the beginning and end of every row until there are 64 stitches. All remaining stitches on every row work in stocking stitch (begin with a purl row)

5 Increase 1 stitch, knit 10, knit 2 together (10 times), knit 11, knit 2 together (10 times), knit 11

6 Cast off purlwise.

7 Cut the yarn from the ball and weave in the ends.

* Block the piece by laying a piece of kitchen towel over it and using a cool iron to steam. Allow the piece to dry.

button loop

Finger knit (or crochet) a 4cm (1.5") long chain. Stitch the ends of the button loop to one pointy end of the shawl. Stitch a decorative/vintage button in place opposite the loop. Wrap the shawl around the shoulders and fasten with the button.

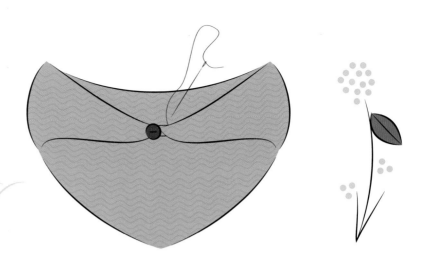

knitted bag

1 Cast on 19 stitches

2 Knit 1 purl 1 until you have knitted 55 rows.

3 Cast off.

* Block the piece by laying a piece of kitchen towel over it and using a cool iron to steam. Allow the piece to dry.

4 Fold the piece in half and mattress stitch the row ends together.

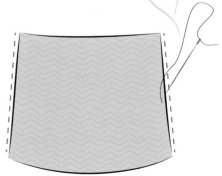

twisted tie strap

1 Cut three 70cm (27.5")
lengths of matching yarn.

2 Tape the three ends to a
tabletop and twist the yarn
until it is very firm.

3 Remove from the tabletop
and fold the piece in half
and let it twist back on itself.
Smooth it out and knot the
end.

4 Stitch the folded end to
one top edge of the bag
opening and the knotted end
to the opposite edge of the
bag opening. Stitch a small
decorative button on top of
the folded end of the strap.

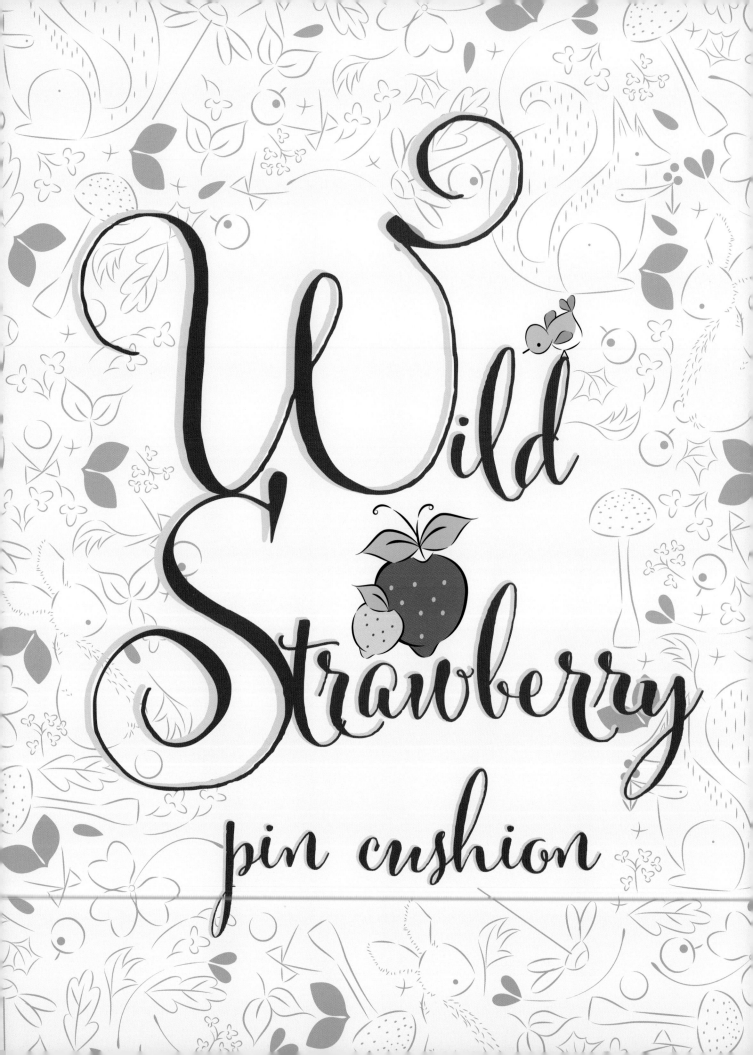

Wild Strawberry

pin cushion

WILD STRAWBERRY PIN CUSHION

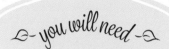

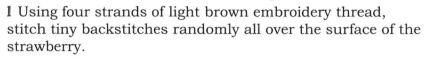

~ you will need ~

- 13" x 7" (33cm x 18cm) 'Mallee' 100% wool hand dyed felt for large strawberry
- 7" x 4" (18cm x 10cm) 'Ginger' 100% wool felt for small strawberry
- 3" x 2.5" (8cm x 6cm) 'Peppercorn' 100% wool hand dyed felt for tiny strawberry
- 9" x 9" (23cm x 23cm) 'Meadow' 100% wool hand dyed felt for leaves
- 9" x 9" (23cm x 23cm) 'Light Green' 100% wool hand dyed felt for leaves
- Dark Brown, Light Brown embroidery thread
- Dark Green Perle Cotton thread
- Embroidery thread for the twisted ties
- Sewing machine thread to match the felt
- Toy fill
- General sewing supplies

* 3mm (1/8") seam allowance included
* templates on page 126 - 127
* finished size
   Large 15cm (6")
   Small 7cm (2¾")
   Tiny 2.5cm (1")

large strawberry

1 Using four strands of light brown embroidery thread, stitch tiny backstitches randomly all over the surface of the strawberry.

2 Using two strands of the same colour thread, stitch tiny French knots on top of one end of each tiny backstitch.

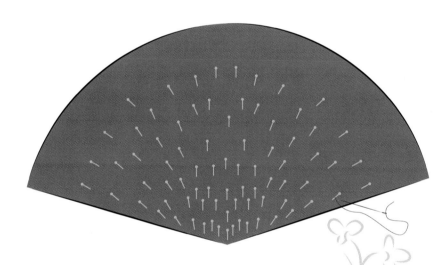

3 With right sides together, fold the large strawberry piece in half, machine stitch along the straight edge. Turn right side out.

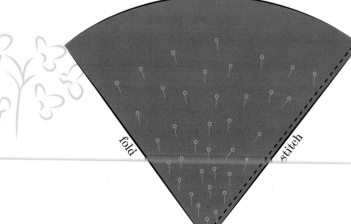

4 Using two strands of matching thread to the strawberry, gather by hand around the top edge.

6 Using one strand of dark green Perle thread, stitch long backstitches randomly around the top opening of the strawberry.

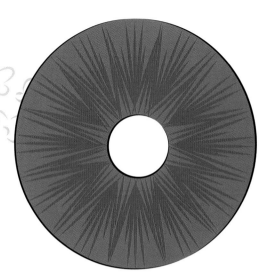

stuffing

← gather →

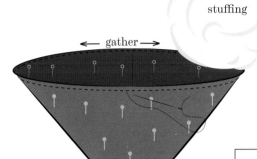

5 Stuff the strawberry well, pull up the gathers towards the middle and fasten off, (don't cut the thread yet, there will be a small opening in the centre). Stuff a little more so your strawberry is nice and firm.

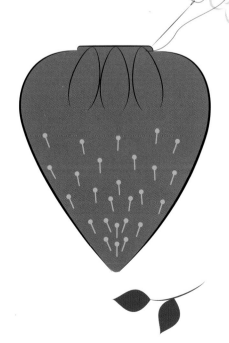

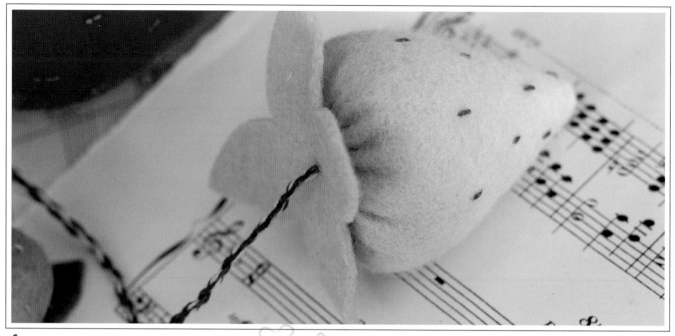

leaves

1 Cut six leaves from light green felt and six from dark green felt. Place them in six groups of two, each group having one light green and one dark green.

3 Fold the straight end of each leaf in half and add a tiny stitch to hold.

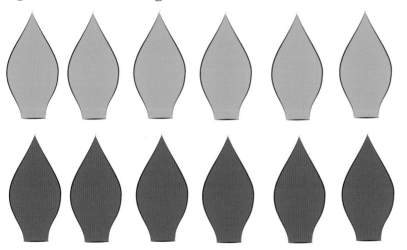

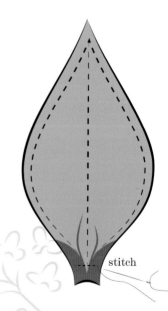

stitch

2 Using a dark green thread on your sewing machine, top stitch all the way around the edge of each leaf. Then top stitch one long line of stitching through the centre of each leaf. Trim the edges of each leaf if needed to keep them neat.

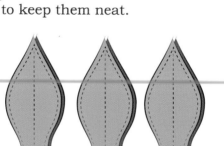

4 Stitch the leaves together at the folded end.

small strawberry

1 Using two strands of brown embroidery thread, stitch tiny backstitches all over the surface of the strawberry.

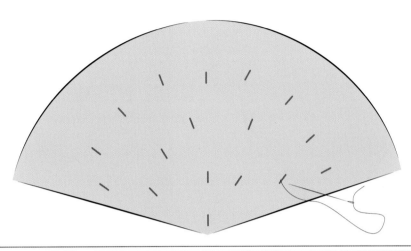

5 Place the folded end of the group of leaves inside the opening, use the length of thread to stitch the leaves in place. Fasten off.

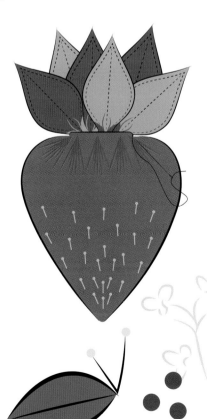

2 With right sides together, fold it in half, machine stitch along the straight edge. Turn right side out.

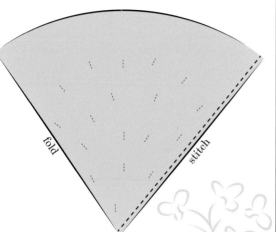

3 Using two strands of matching thread to the strawberry, gather by hand around the top edge.

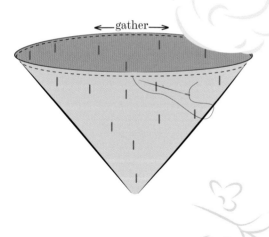

4 Stuff the strawberry well, pull up the gathers and fasten off. (Don't cut the thread as yet)

5 Cut out one medium strawberry leaf. Stitch it in place on the top of the strawberry with a tiny back stitch.

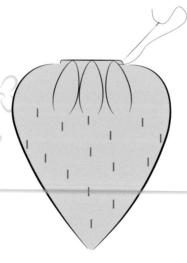

tiny strawberry

1 Make one tiny strawberry in the same way as the small strawberry, using a small leaf for the top.

twisted tie

1 Cut four 50cm (20") lengths of three matching coloured embroidery threads, (12 strands in total).

2 Tape the ends to a tabletop and twist the thread until it is very firm.

3 Remove from the tabletop and fold the piece in half and let it twist back on itself. Smooth it out and knot the ends together.

4 Stitch the folded end to the top of the small strawberry.

5 Make another twisted tie in the same way that is 35cm (14") long and stitch it to the top of the tiny strawberry.

6 Stitch the knotted ends of both ties to the centre of the large strawberry.

109

Templates

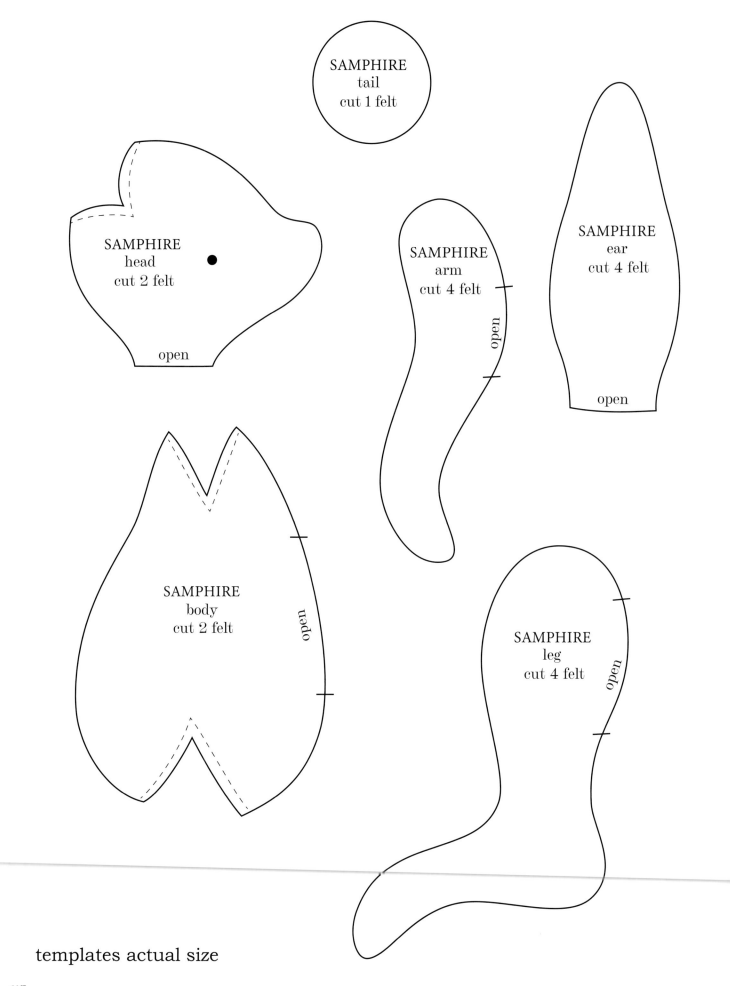

SAMPHIRE
tail
cut 1 felt

SAMPHIRE
head
cut 2 felt

open

SAMPHIRE
arm
cut 4 felt

open

SAMPHIRE
ear
cut 4 felt

open

SAMPHIRE
body
cut 2 felt

open

SAMPHIRE
leg
cut 4 felt

open

templates actual size

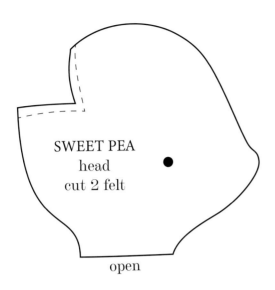

SWEET PEA
head
cut 2 felt

open

SWEET PEA
ears
cut 2 felt
cut 2 fabric

open

open

gather

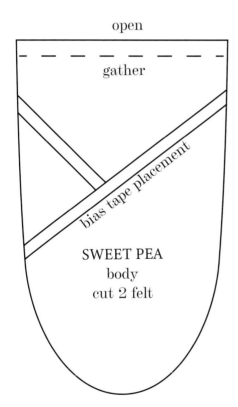

bias tape placement

SWEET PEA
body
cut 2 felt

SWEET PEA   tail   cut 1 felt

templates actual size

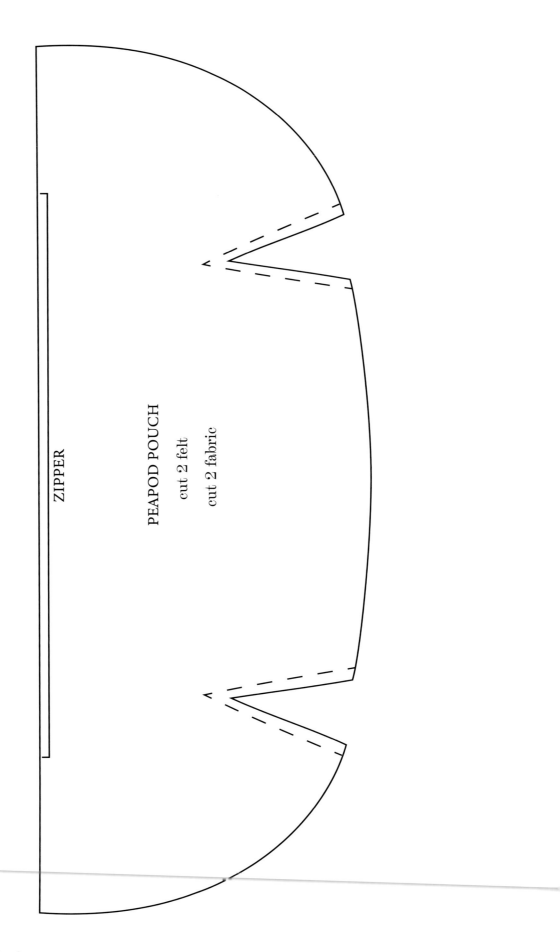

ZIPPER

PEAPOD POUCH

cut 2 felt

cut 2 fabric

templates actual size

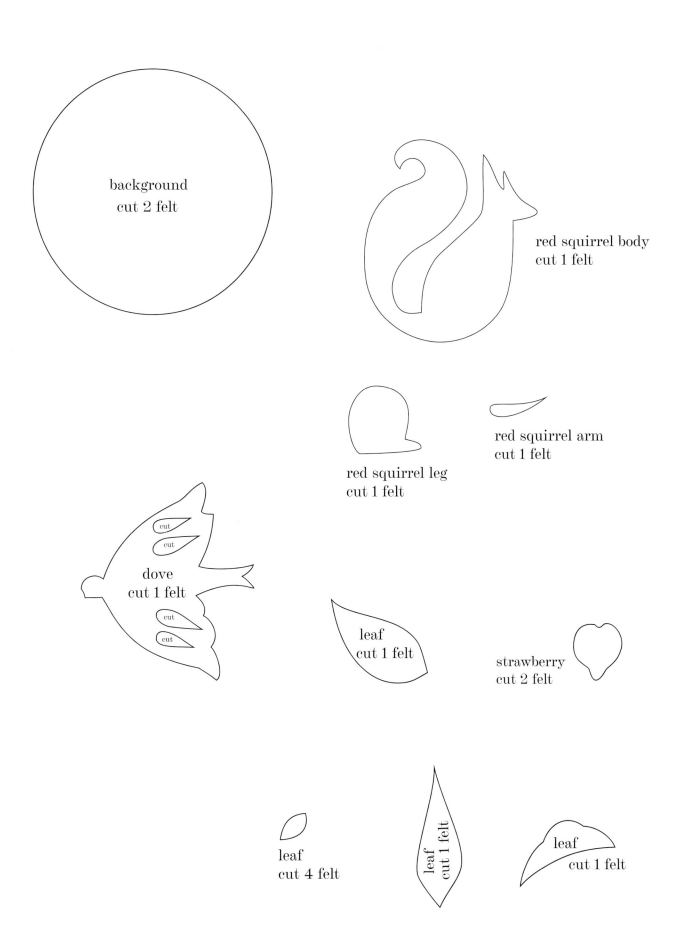

background
cut 2 felt

red squirrel body
cut 1 felt

red squirrel leg
cut 1 felt

red squirrel arm
cut 1 felt

cut
cut

dove
cut 1 felt

cut
cut

leaf
cut 1 felt

strawberry
cut 2 felt

leaf
cut 4 felt

leaf
cut 1 felt

leaf
cut 1 felt

templates actual size

BLACKTHORN FOREST BROOCHES
PLACEMENT GUIDE

templates actual size

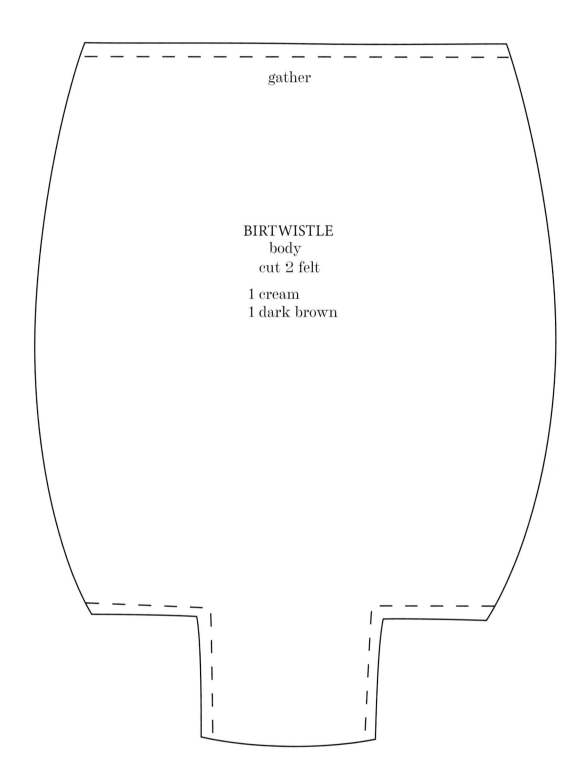

gather

BIRTWISTLE
body
cut 2 felt

1 cream
1 dark brown

templates actual size

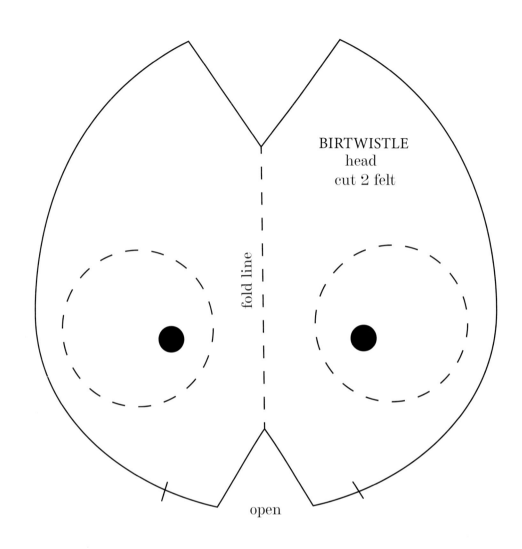

BIRTWISTLE
head
cut 2 felt

fold line

open

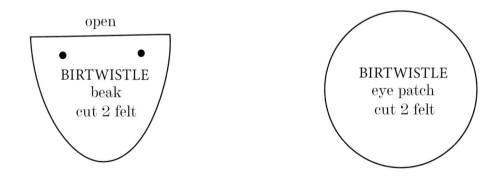

open

BIRTWISTLE
beak
cut 2 felt

BIRTWISTLE
eye patch
cut 2 felt

templates actual size

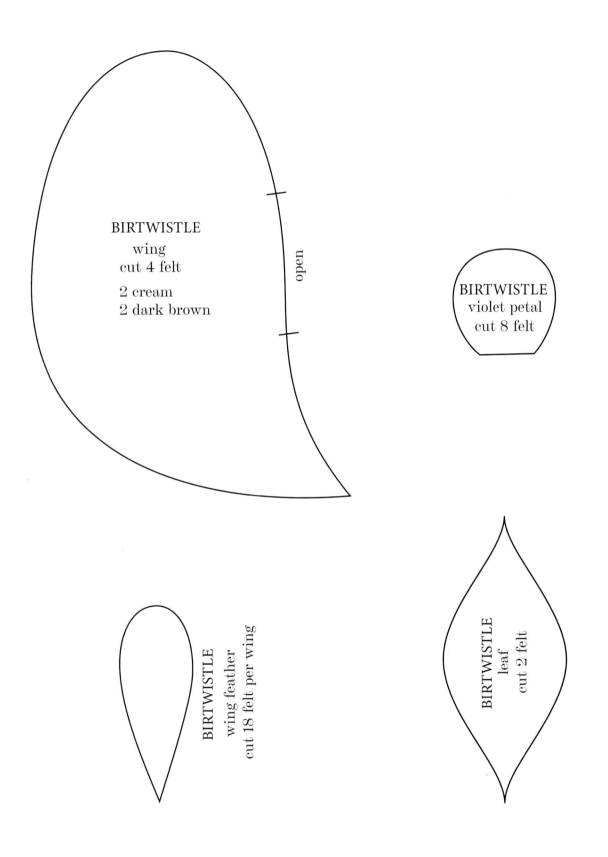

BIRTWISTLE
wing
cut 4 felt

2 cream
2 dark brown

open

BIRTWISTLE
violet petal
cut 8 felt

BIRTWISTLE
wing feather
cut 18 felt per wing

BIRTWISTLE
leaf
cut 2 felt

templates actual size

WOODLAND HEATH
mini quilt
cut 1 felt

LEAF cut 16 fabric

templates actual size

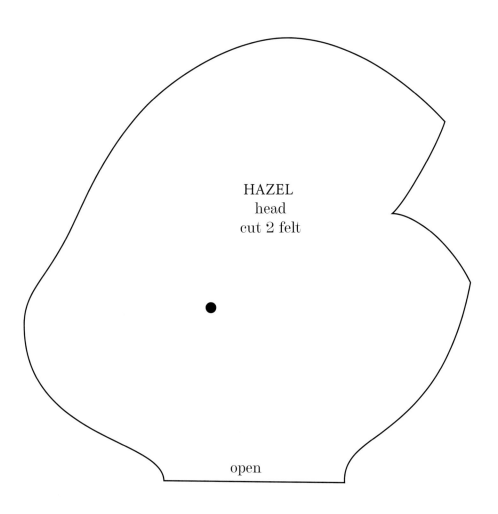

HAZEL
head
cut 2 felt

open

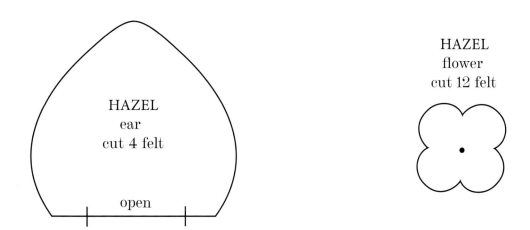

HAZEL
ear
cut 4 felt

open

HAZEL
flower
cut 12 felt

templates actual size

123

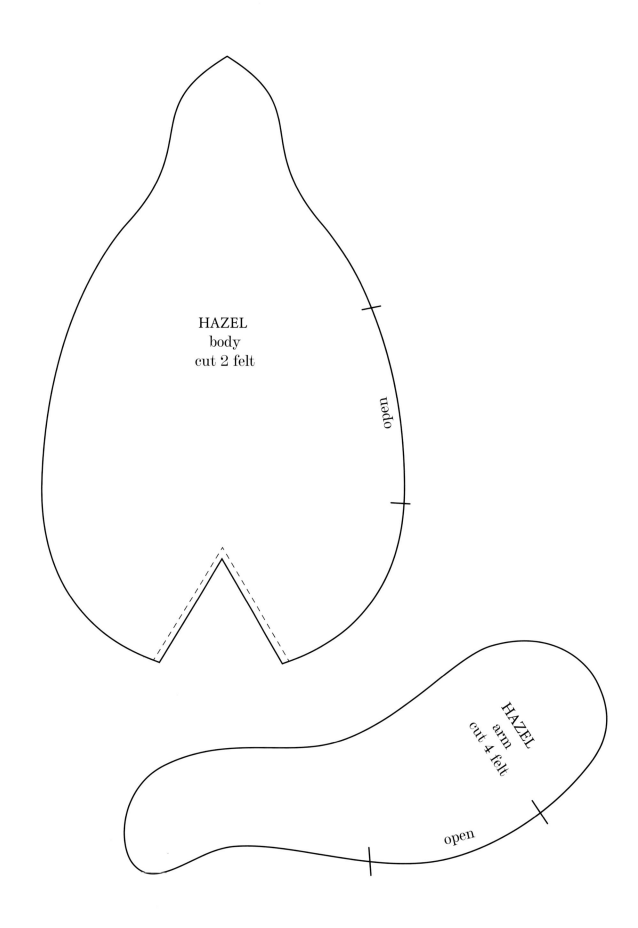

HAZEL
body
cut 2 felt

open

HAZEL
arm
cut 4 felt

open

templates actual size

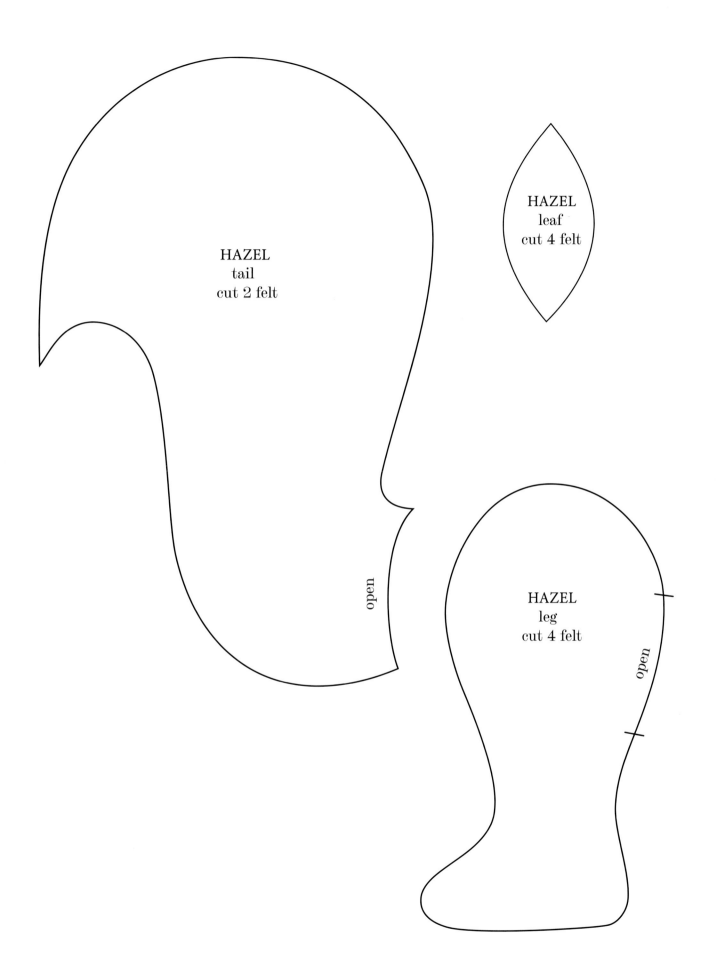

HAZEL
tail
cut 2 felt

HAZEL
leaf
cut 4 felt

open

HAZEL
leg
cut 4 felt

open

templates actual size

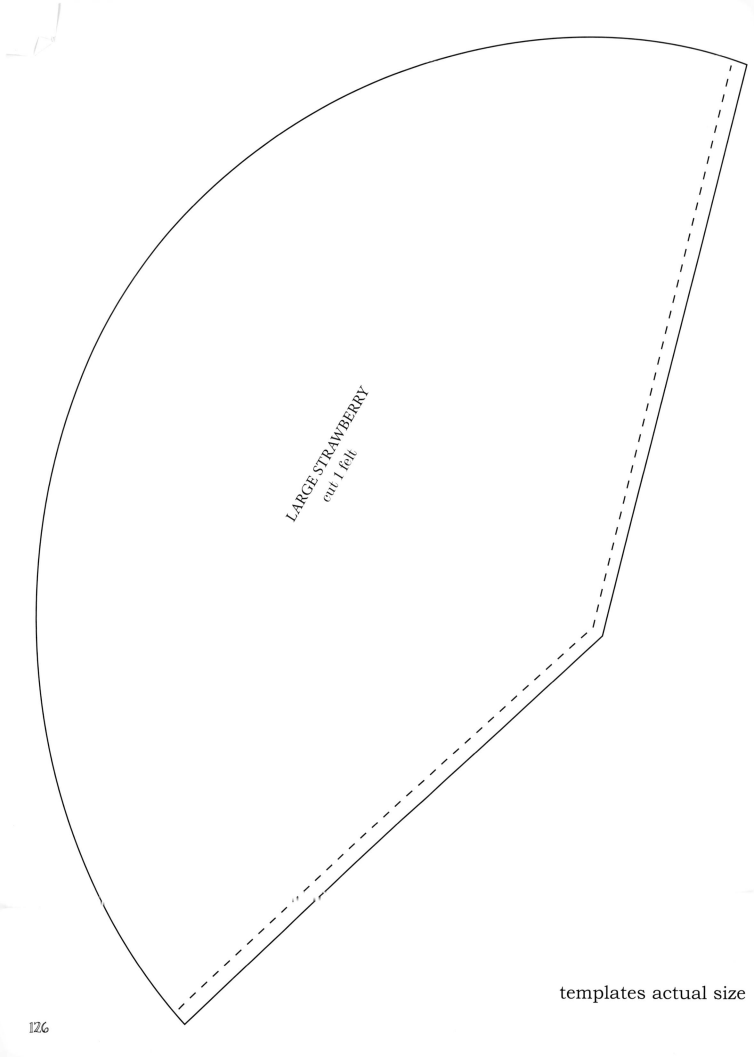

LARGE STRAWBERRY
cut 1 felt

templates actual size

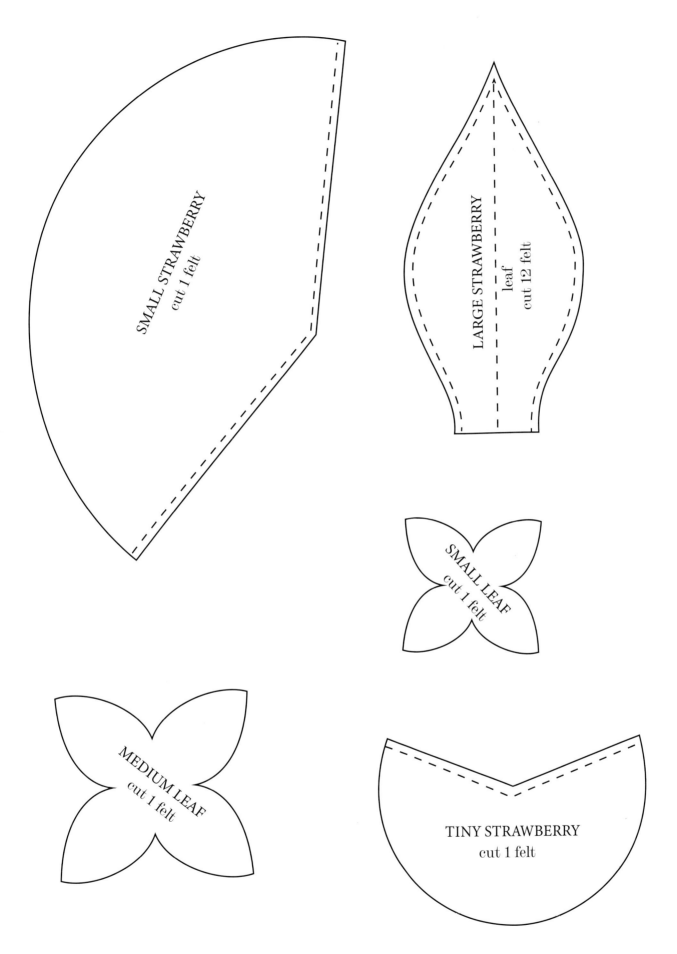

SMALL STRAWBERRY
cut 1 felt

LARGE STRAWBERRY
leaf
cut 12 felt

SMALL LEAF
cut 1 felt

MEDIUM LEAF
cut 1 felt

TINY STRAWBERRY
cut 1 felt

templates actual size

Suppliers

felt and felt balls

Winterwood
www.winterwoodtoys.com.au

haemostats

May Blossom Store
www.etsy.com/au/shop/MayBlossomStore

cross stitch fabric

www.etsy.com

linen

The Fabric Store
www.wearethefabricstore.com

eyes

Bear Essence
www.bearessence.com.au

yarn

Jamieson's of Shetland
www.jamiesonsofshetland.co.uk

embroidery thread

Cosmo Embroidery Thread
www.etsy.com

buttons

Vintage
www.etsy.com and my own collection